D0934487

St. Margaret Middle School Library
1716-A Churchville Road
Bel Air, Maryland 21015

Everything You Need to Know About

ABUSIVE RELATIONSHIPS

St. Margaret Middle School Library
1716-A Churchville Road
Bel Air, Maryland 21015

Early in a relationship, you may not know if your partner is abusive.

Everything You Need to Know About

ABUSIVE RELATIONSHIPS

Nancy N. Rue

THE ROSEN PUBLISHING GROUP, INC.
NEW YORK

Published in 1996, 1998 by The Rosen Publishing Group, Inc.
29 East 21st Street, New York, NY 10010

Revised Edition 1998

Copyright © 1996, 1998 by The Rosen Publishing Group, Inc.

All rights reserved. No part of this book may be reproduced in any form without permission in writing from the publisher, except by a reviewer.

Library of Congress Cataloging-in-Publication Data

Rue, Nancy N.
     Everything you need to know about abusive relationships / Nancy N. Rue.
          p.   cm — (The need to know library)
     ISBN 0-8239-2832-2
     Includes bibliographical references and index.
     Summary: Discusses different kinds of abuse that occur between teens who are dating and offers advice on how to handle abusive situations.
     1. Dating violence—United States—Juvenile literature. 2. Teenagers—Abuse of—United States—Juvenile literature. [1. Dating violence.] I. Title. II. Series.
HQ801.83.R86   1996
306.73'0835—dc20   95-24743
                                                                                          CIP
                                                                                          AC

Manufactured in the United States of America

Contents

Introduction

*D*ean was Pam's first serious boyfriend. He was a year older and played varsity basketball. He had a great sense of humor and seemed to know everyone. Suddenly people knew who Pam was too.

Dean had dated other girls, but Pam was different. He took her to parties and made sure everyone knew she was with him. He made her feel important.

Pam spent most of her time with Dean and had not been seeing her friends as usual. One Friday after school Dean called to tell her what time the basketball game started and about the party being held after the game. She said that she had already made plans with friends. He told her that none of the other guys' girlfriends ever missed a game and that she better be there. Then Dean hung up on her.

Pam was puzzled, but she didn't call back. She kept her plans with her friends, although she felt a little guilty.

When Pam came home, Dean was waiting at her door. She was relieved to see him and ran across the lawn toward him. Instead of hugging her, he grabbed her by the hair, demanding to know where she had been and whom she had been with. Pam could hardly speak.

Dean let her go. Then he shouted that she didn't know what it was like for him not knowing where she was all night. Pam felt angry and confused as well as a bit surprised by how upset she had made him. They took a walk and she talked to him until he calmed down. He felt badly for yelling and grabbing her. He apologized profusely and Pam forgave him.

In the next few weeks, Dean began questioning Pam as to where she was when they weren't together. He didn't like her speaking with other guys and often accused her of flirting. Pam often found Dean pulling her aside at parties and squeezing her arm tightly while he scolded her for "flirting." Sometimes he squeezed her so hard that he left bruises in the shape of his fingers on her arms. Pam thought that Dean's jealousy was so intense because of their intense feelings for each other.

One night, while walking with a group of friends, Dean and Pam had a disagreement. As they neared Pam's house, Dean told his friends to go on ahead. As soon as they were alone, Pam recognized the familiar look of fury in Dean's eyes. He told her she had made him look stupid in front of his friends. Pam told him he was being ridiculous. Then, Dean slapped her across the face. He hit her again and again.

Pam was shocked. She wanted only to get away from him and into her house. She knew that if she screamed, her parents would hear her and help her. Still, she was afraid to call out for help. When his tirade finally ended, Dean and Pam were both crying. He held her very close and said he was sorry over and over.

The abuse in this situation may seem obvious to you, but it isn't always always clear to those involved in the relationship. Recognizing abusive behavior and not accepting it is essential for all teens who are dating or who plan to date.

On the average, about one out of every three high school students is or has been involved in an abusive dating relationship. There are 700,000 assaults on women each year, and two-thirds of the victims are under the age of eighteen.

These women may have been called horrible names or told they were worthless. They might have been threatened with violence or had their possessions destroyed. Or perhaps they've actually been pushed, slapped, kicked, punched, or even had a knife held to their throat—all in the name of love.

No matter what the situation, this type of behavior is called abuse. This book is about abuse, and it's for everyone who is or will be in a romantic relationship.

For this book to help you, you need to understand the basic rules it is based on.

The Basic Rules

Abuse is never okay. Whatever the reason, it is not right for people in a relationship to hurt each other with words, actions, physical force, or sex.

It makes no difference whether the abuser is unhappy, stressed out, or drunk; his or her abuse is never justifiable. Abuse should not be tolerated, ignored, or brushed aside. There may be apologies. But once someone uses abuse and gets away with it, he or she will do it again and again if they aren't made to seek help or if the victim doesn't leave the relationship.

Many of the abusers we'll be talking about are guys, but it's important to realize that girls can be and are abusive too.

Violence is not a healthy expression of anger and may be a sign that someone is trying to control you.

Chapter 1

What Is an Abusive Relationship?

*J*ason and Stephanie were in the library working *on a project for English class. They were laughing and joking—until Stephanie's boyfriend, Nick, came in and saw them. Nick marched over to them and slammed his fist down on their table.*

"What the hell's this?" he shouted at Stephanie. "I can't trust you for a minute!"

While everyone in the library watched in horror, Nick grabbed Stephanie by the arm and dragged her to the door. By the time they got outside, Stephanie was shaking. She said to Nick, "Okay, if you don't want me to talk to Jason anymore, I won't. I'll get Mrs. Anderson to give me another partner for the project."

Right away, Nick felt better. He even told Stephanie he was sorry for getting a "little upset." Stephanie breathed a huge sigh of relief. Everything was all right now.

Excessive jealousy and possessiveness are often an early warning sign that your boyfriend or girlfriend is abusive.

But of course, it wasn't.

Nick and Stephanie were already in an abusive relationship. It wasn't just a "stormy romance." What was happening between them could be called violence, abuse, or battering—and it was dangerous.

Every relationship has conflicts. That's normal. No two people can spend a lot of time together without disagreeing on something. For example, if Nick and Stephanie couldn't agree on what movie to see, they could argue about it all evening, but they wouldn't be violent or abusive. No one would be hurt.

But when Stephanie did something that upset Nick, he set out to hurt her. He wanted to control and dominate her. That's abuse. That's violence. Let's spell it out very carefully.

Abuse is when someone uses force on purpose to gain power over another person. Abuse is meant to frighten another person.

Emotional Abuse

A violent relationship usually begins with emotional abuse. That is what Nick was using on Stephanie. It's any action that causes fear in another person. It's anything that makes a girl or boy feel powerless against a boyfriend or girlfriend.

Let's look at some examples of emotional abuse in a dating relationship:

- Driving a car recklessly to scare the person
- Going through personal belongings without permission
- Destroying things that are important to the person
- Criticizing him or her, especially in front of others
- Not allowing a girlfriend to spend time with her other friends; resenting the time a boyfriend spends with his family
- Constantly telling someone how to act and speak.

Those kinds of actions are considered abuse. They can destroy something very valuable—a person's self-esteem. If a girl is constantly told in words and actions that she is ugly or stupid, she begins to believe it.

Physical Abuse

When Heather was dating Brent, everything was wonderful at first. He was the first guy who had ever sent her flowers or written her poems. When he started pouting because she talked to other guys or wanted to spend a Friday night with her girlfriends, she thought it was because he loved her so much.

But after a while that got old. Heather loved to go on camping trips with her family. She had male friends she'd known since kindergarten. She even liked to be by herself sometimes and paint or read. When Brent couldn't handle that, she decided to break up with him.

Heather had broken up with guys before. She didn't think she was doing anything dangerous by waiting until they were alone in a parked car to tell him. But when she did, he threw open the passenger door and shoved her out onto the ground. Then he hurled himself on top of her, screaming words like "slut" and "whore," and punched her in the stomach over and over. She doesn't know what would have happened if a couple in another car hadn't heard her cries and chased Brent off.

The first time a boy or girl abuses his or her companion, it usually isn't as severe as what Brent did to Heather. In the beginning, the abuse usually takes the form of:

- "Play fighting"—wrestling that gets a little too rough, and one person seems to enjoy it too much
- A little punch that was meant to hurt; if the girl complains, the boy usually says, "Oh, come on, I didn't hit you that hard."
- A pinch
- A yank on a handful of hair
- A slap in the face

If the abused person doesn't leave when this starts, it usually gets worse. It can turn into:

- Punching, kicking, or biting
- Pushing or throwing someone across a room, down stairs, or against a wall
- Burning the person with something, like a cigarette or a car cigarette lighter
- Choking

When we see a lot of violence on TV or in the movies, we get used to it. We forget that violence is real. When a girl is abused by her boyfriend, she can suffer broken bones and burns. She might suffer a concussion, bloody nose, bruises, and black eyes.

Sometimes no physical marks are left after a violent scene. Maybe the boy grabs his girlfriend's wrist and drags her someplace she doesn't want to go. Maybe he pushes her down and won't let her up until she promises never to talk to another boy again.

It doesn't matter whether she ends up in the hospital or not. If a person uses physical force against another—no matter how minor it seems—that's violence. That's abuse.

Sexual Abuse

Rebecca did not want to sleep with Matthew. She had made that clear to him a dozen times. But every time they went out, he pressured her to have sex.

At first, Rebecca thought it was kind of flattering. She never dreamed he would try to force her.

One night when he took her home and walked her to the door, she said, "You can't come in. My parents aren't home." As she unlocked the door, Matthew shoved her inside. Locking the door behind him, he pushed Rebecca against the wall.

"Come on," he said. "It'll be incredible."

Pressing her hard against the wall, he reached down and shoved his other hand between her legs. She kept crying out, "No! Stop it!" but Matthew kept on.

Finally, Rebecca bit his arm and he let go.

"You don't have to be such a bitch!" he told her.

Rebecca opened the door and said, "Get out."

He did. Then Rebecca slid to the floor and cried. But tears couldn't wash away her terrible sense of shame.

If someone uses force, threats, or insults to make someone do something sexual against his or her will, it is sexual abuse.

Even though Matthew didn't rape her, Rebecca was sexually abused. Abuse means forcing someone to do something against one's will.

Every person should have control over his or her own body. When a girl feels fear or shame because of what someone is trying to make her do with her body, she is being sexually abused.

When we think of sexual abuse in a dating relationship, we think of date rape. One third of all rapes committed in the United States are by a girl's own date or boyfriend. The peak age for that kind of rape to occur is sixteen for boys, and fourteen for girls.

Rape is not the only kind of sexual abuse that

can happen on a date. Anything connected with sex that brings out feelings of shame, disgust, or fear is sexual abuse. Some examples:

- Someone who constantly pushes for more sexually
- Using threats to go further
- Using insults to get the person to sleep with him or her
- Threatening with violence if the person doesn't do what the other wants.

Sexual abuse, then, is any form of sexual contact that is hurtful and forceful. If it brings shame and depression and guilt, it's abuse.

Date rape is a severe form of sexual abuse. It would seem easy for someone to know if he or she had been raped, but when it happens with a partner, the issue becomes cloudy. "I know him," she may think. "We've done some pretty heavy kissing before. Maybe he felt it was okay."

The point is, if someone forces sexual intercourse on another person, it's rape, even if:

- They know each other
- They've dated for a long time
- They've touched in personal ways
- One or both of them are drunk
- They've had sex before.

How to Know If It's Abuse

When a person is involved in a violent

relationship with someone he or she really cares about, it's sometimes hard to see that it is abusive. It's also very difficult to admit. So much shame is involved, often for both people.

The first step in stopping violence is facing it. The following list can help a girl take stock of her own relationship. If she answers yes to more than five of these questions, she's a victim of abuse. If she answers yes to any of them, she needs to take a look at the relationship.

- I'm confused about my relationship. My boyfriend says he loves me, but he doesn't act that way.
- I am afraid of him.
- I can't express my feelings without being afraid of what he will say or do.
- He snoops into my personal belongings.
- I always ask him for permission to spend time with my friends.
- I am always trying to make everything perfect for him so he won't get mad.
- Sometimes he acts as if he's doing me a favor by dating him.
- He has hit, slapped, pushed, or kicked me before.
- I feel that he is trying to run my life.
- My friends say "Break up with him."

Now you know what makes up an abusive relationship. Now, remember the ground rules:

Abuse can include having the privacy of one's personal belongings violated.

- Violence is an unhealthy, dangerous way of dealing with feelings. It is never okay.
- No one should have to put up with abuse.
- Abuse never goes away by itself.

Those ground rules seem simple. But many people don't believe them—they have learned things about violence and abuse that are false.

Chapter 2

Myths About Abuse

If we are ever to put an end to violence in relationships, we have to teach people that certain myths, or made-up stories, are false. Let's explore some of them along with the facts.

Myth #1: In a perfect, fairy-tale romance, the boy takes care of the girl, so he should be in control of the relationship.

Fact: There is no such thing as a perfect, fairy-tale romance. In the old stories, brave men rescued helpless women, but it doesn't work that way. But if a girl or guy believes that, he or she is also likely to believe that it's okay for a man to beat up a woman because he's in charge of the relationship.

Myth #2: If the boy isn't in charge of the relationship, the girl is. Somebody has to be.

Fact: Human relationships are not about control. They're about two people working out their differences. If one person feels that he or she has to be in charge, there's force in the relationship and there could be abuse.

For a relationship to work, both of the people involved have to work together.

Myth #3: Love is when two people are so crazy about each other that they can't stand to be apart.

Fact: If a boy like Nick is possessive and jealous, it isn't because of how much he loves Stephanie. It's because he needs someone else to make him feel secure and empower him. With real love, two people enjoy being together, but they also take time to be with other people or by themselves.

Abuse can enter a relationship when one person thinks he or she can't live without the other. A boy like Brent will do anything to hold on to his girlfriend, including beating her. A girl like Heather, who is independent and has outside interests, won't tolerate outrageous circumstances, including abuse, just to sustain a relationship.

Myth #4: Some guys simply have bad tempers. A girl who dates a guy like this just has to learn how to communicate with him properly.

Fact: Abuse isn't a communication problem. It's an anger problem. People like this don't just have "bad tempers." They needs professional help.

Myth # 5: It's okay to hit a girl if she hits you.

Fact: A girl has no more right to hit her boyfriend when she is angered by his actions than he has to hit her. But even if she does, that doesn't give him the right to hit her back. No one should accept being hit, but the smart way to deal with it is to walk away and cool off.

Myth # 6: Some girls like to be slapped around. That's why they stay in abusive relationships.

Fact: No one likes to be purposefully hurt, particularly by someone who says "I love you."

Myth # 7: A guy can't help it if he hits a girl, especially if he's drunk. He's out of control.

Fact: Dean always made sure that no one else saw him abuse Pam. He would either discreetly squeeze her arm or wait until the end of the night when the two of them were alone. Pam realized that Dean knew what he was doing.

An abuser hits someone to gain control, not because of their lack of control.

We can't just wipe out these myths by saying, "That's not true." We have to replace them with things that are true.

Chapter 3

Why Would Someone Who "Loves" You Abuse You?

A person makes a choice to be violent, but why? The following are some of the reasons. They come from batterers themselves: men and women who have used violence on the ones they dated, loved, and married.

Reason #1: It works.

Paula was dating Jesse. He was smart and had a quick tongue. She was slower to express herself. Whenever they had an argument, Jesse could almost always out-talk her. One night she got so mad when he was talking circles around her that she just slapped him. He stopped, stunned. Suddenly, the fight was over, and Paula felt she had won. The next time they started to quarrel, Jesse wasn't so quick to lash out at her. Paula believed that abuse worked for her.

Whenever something works to make us feel better, we want to do it again. That's why people get hooked on drugs or alcohol.

Reason #2: They're trying to live up to an image.

There isn't a person in the world who doesn't at some time feel weak and out of control. If we were brought up to believe that we can never make mistakes, or never be afraid, we'd be in trouble. No one can possibly live up to that.

The one who tries to be all these things will have to seek power in relationships. Eventually there will be some emotion other than anger, like fear. But this person can only express it as anger.

Reason #3: Violence satisfies the need for control.

Most teenagers need some control in their lives, but most find positive ways to achieve it. They may do well in school. They may excel in sports or get a job. If they don't find positive ways, they'll find negative ones. Abuse is one of those ways.

Reason #4: The person depends too much on his or her girlfriend or boyfriend.

Javier often felt sad because he was growing up without a father, and his mother was dating a man he couldn't stand. It was normal for Javier to feel disappointed and anxious, but he didn't see it that way. He thought he was supposed to "deal with it."

One of the reasons he loved being with Elena was that she understood him so well. After a while, he expected her to know how he felt and how to make him feel better. In fact, he even began to blame her whenever he felt lousy.

Violence on television or in movies may lead some people to think that using violence is an acceptable way of solving problems.

She became so much a part of him that whenever she talked to anyone else he got scared. What if she left him? What would he do?

Javier started to demand that Elena sit in the restaurant where he worked and wait for him to finish his shift. He put down her friends and told her not to hang around with them. Soon, Elena had nothing in her life except Javier; she was as dependent on him as he was on her. He liked it that way, so he worked even harder to hold onto her and control her.

Those are the main reasons why people become abusive. Other things can add to those reasons and make abuse easier to choose.

Emotions of jealousy, guilt, fear, or confusion can fuel abusive incidents. Often our society shows violence as the best way to deal with these feelings.

As children, we grow up with superhero idols that teach us might is right. We also live in a culture that is highly competitive, a value often instilled in children. The combination of the two can affect how a person deals with conflict. Film, television, and music often glamorize anger and aggression.

Violence in the Media

Seeing violence on television doesn't make someone an abuser. It just makes it easier to decide that it's okay to do it.

Violence on television has increased by 65 percent since 1980. By age eighteen, the average person has seen 50,000 murders or attempted murders on TV alone. That doesn't include violent porno magazines, rock videos, and bloody movies that can be seen at home. Many of those combine violence with sex—and depict the women involved as eager participants.

Violence in Music

Music is one of the most popular forms of expression for teens. Rap music has been the fastest-growing genre of music to date. It is listened to almost exclusively by teens. A survey of rap music reported that 78 percent of rap lyrics made references to violence.

Violence in Sports

Sports are supposed to be a healthy way to expend

extra energy, and many times they are. But they can also act like gasoline on a fire to a person who is already prone to violence. In the football locker room a guy often hears, "Get out there and tear them up!" or "Kill the quarterback!" He learns to release anxiety by playing rough. It works—and he may use it elsewhere.

He also finds out that somebody has to win—and it had better be him. If no one teaches him otherwise, that may carry over into his relationships.

That doesn't mean that sports are bad. Not every high school football player beats up his girlfriend. But if no one teaches him that this kind of roughness needs to be left on the field, he could be in trouble.

Violence in the Family

Many kids have seen their fathers hit their mothers for years on end. The kids themselves may have been beaten by their fathers too. These kids might feel that along with physical traits, they have inherited their violent natures from their fathers.

It is true that abusive children often come from violent homes. Many have parents who aren't batterers, but who have little respect for each other or haven't shown their kids positive ways to express emotions.

Abusive kids may have hated seeing their mothers abused, but abusing someone else gives them the power they never had while they stood by helplessly. Other kids watched their dads batter their mothers and grew up thinking that behavior is acceptable within a romantic relationship.

So much of what we do has been modeled by our parents. Violence often breeds more violence.

This is especially true of emotional abuse. Many parents discipline their kids with yelling and screaming. If it isn't wrong to scream horrible things at someone you love, why should it be wrong to scream horrible things at your boyfriend or girlfriend?

Other Family Problems

Dean did not grow up in a violent family. His parents divorced when he was eleven and his mother remarried a year later. His father did not keep in contact with the family, and Dean had not seen him in years.

Dean's stepfather was a stern man who seemed to notice Dean only when he did something wrong. Dean felt as though his mother had abandoned him because she would never interfere or defend him.

Forty percent of all young people in the United States will see their parents go through a divorce before they're eighteen. Because of this, they will feel more stress. They may be more likely to get involved with alcohol or drugs. They may be more likely to commit suicide, get in trouble with the law, or fail in school. These are all things that make violence come easier.

If a boy becomes abusive, it's because he chooses to be abusive. He must accept responsibility for this and seek help if he hopes to end the violence in his life.

But once a boy has been abusive to his girlfriend, she also has a problem. She's now in a dangerous relationship. Why would she stay in the relationship?

Chapter 4

Why People Stay in Abusive Relationships

*A*manda thought she had died and gone to heaven when she started going with Robbie. He was almost too good to be true.

He was president of the student body. He was the star of the soccer team. And he was really handsome. A lot of other girls were dying to date him.

But he had chosen her.

He did everything for her, from checking out books for her from the library to picking out her makeup so she'd look perfect. But all of this had a price tag.

If she disagreed with him, he walked away mad. If she wanted to do something on her own, he gave her the silent treatment. If she didn't give him all her attention when they were with other people, he announced that they were leaving.

When there was an opening in the student council, Amanda decided to run for it. She thought Robbie would be proud of her. But when he found out, he was furious. He accused her of using him to "climb to the top." When she argued with him about this, he slapped her across the face.

The next day, Amanda withdrew her name from the race. That afternoon, a dozen red roses were delivered to her house with a card from Robbie saying, "I'm sorry about what happened."

The next two weeks were like a honeymoon: presents, cards, and endless affection from Robbie.

But soon it was time for finals and Robbie was stressed. For a reason Amanda can't even remember, Robbie pulled out a clump of her hair while he was yelling at her. After a few more incidents, Amanda finally admitted to herself that she was in trouble.

So she left him, right?

Wrong.

In fact, only about four out of ten relationships end after the onset of violence or abuse and only one out of every twenty-five victims seek help.

As the victim in an abusive relationship, Amanda went through much inner turmoil. What she discovered is that no matter how easy an outsider may think it is to leave, it's never that simple for a victim. The reasons to stay seem too big to get around:

Reason #1: She's ashamed.

When someone purposefully hurts you, it can make you feel horrible about yourself. Amanda looked around at other girls her age with their boyfriends and thought, "Why is this happening to me?" It's embarrassing, so

Amanda tried to hide it. It's too scary to face, so she pretended that it wasn't there.

Reason #2: She thinks she can change him.

You can't wave a magic wand to make an abuser stop. Those who abuse others have to face the problem that lies within themselves.

Reason #3: She thinks the battering is her fault.

Pam believed that she didn't know how to act in a relationship. She thought that if she were able to make Dean happy he would stop hurting her.

If someone has been raised with a strong sense of responsibility, it is natural for that person to think that when things go wrong, he or she is to blame. It is difficult for the victim to believe that the abuser is actually the one with the problem.

Reason #4: She's scared.

When Heather told Brent she wanted to break up with him, he threw her out of a car and beat her up.

Is it any wonder an abused person is afraid?

A number of other things are involved. Let's look at some of them.

Violence in the Family

Elena had been abused by her father while she was growing up. This has caused her to accept Javier's abuse. Of women who witnessed violence at home as children, 66 percent become victims themselves later in life.

For Amanda, violence from Robbie was a shock. She had never been hit as a child, and her parents were

An abused person often feels that it's easier to stay in the abusive
relationship than to leave; many victims are afraid of the
consequences, or think they can even change the abuser.

How a girl is raised by her family may affect her future relationships.

never violent toward each other. She could only think it was happening because of something she had done wrong.

The Way a Child Is Raised

The way that a child is brought up can influence his or her future relationships.

Children who are not given much praise or encouragement might not value their own self-worth. They may have a lack of self-confidence that allows someone else take control of a relationship or of them.

If children are pushed and given too much responsibility, they may grow up feeling they always need to be in control. They may become overly assertive.

Parents often raise their children differently according to gender. Girls are sometimes taught that it's important to be attractive and act passive, often, putting others' needs in front of their own. Boys may be instilled with the belief that they are supposed to protect women and make decisions for them.

What the World Tells You

Many movies send a clear message that violence is the way to solve problems. Commercials and magazine ads often say that men are tough and women are soft. Messages like these can make it difficult for a girl to leave a relationship because of a bruised arm. A girl's own friends may even tell her, "It's not that bad. At least you have a boyfriend."

It is hard to leave. But it can be done, and we will talk about that later. First, let's see how a person can avoid getting involved in an abusive relationship in the first place.

St. Margaret Middle School Library
1716-A Churchville Road
Bel Air, Maryland 21015

Chapter 5

How to Avoid Abuse

*M*arijean's mother studied and wrote about domestic violence and relationship abuse, and Marijean had been hearing about the topic since she was old enough to understand. So not long after she started dating Matt, she saw trouble coming.

The first time they went out, he was fun. She laughed the whole time and thought this might be the start of something really cool.

The next time he took her out, they met her friends at the movies. She sat between Matt and another friend, Luke, and every time she leaned over to say something to Luke, Matt would pull her toward him. He was a little rough, she thought.

The movie got out late, and Matt was afraid he wasn't going to get Marijean home in time to make his own curfew. He became very quiet and drove fast—enough to scare Marijean. When they had to stop for a traffic light, Matt started cussing and *banging on the steering wheel with his fists.*

"It's no big deal," Marijean said. "Just call your parents when we get to my house."

"I can handle it, okay?" he snapped back at her.

Marijean was mad. But when they got to her house, Matt seemed to have forgotten all about it and expected her to make out with him in the driveway. She got scared and ran inside.

The next morning, her mother found a present on the front porch. Marijean opened it to find a clown doll with a tear painted on its cheek and a note saying, "I'm sorry."

Marijean wanted to take the doll and toss it in the trash can. There was something about the way Matt acted that made her uneasy. She didn't want to date him anymore, and when he called, she told him so.

At first Matt begged her to give him another chance. He said he had just been "uptight." When she still refused, he got nasty and called her a bitch before he hung up.

That stung Marijean for a minute. But then she talked to her mom. They decided that she had done the right thing by getting out of the relationship before it started. Matt was sending out all the signals of an abuser.

Marijean followed the four guidelines for avoiding an abusive relationship.

Guideline #1: Learn to love yourself first.

A good relationship is a wonderful thing, but it's important not to think you're "nothing" if you're not in one. All of us need to be sure we can do these things before we're ready to share our lives with someone else:

- Have control over your own life
- Enjoy being alone sometimes
- Don't look down on yourself
- Know what you believe in and what you want
- Feel secure even when you're alone

Guideline #2: Know your rights and stand up for them. You have the right to:

- Share equally in decisions
- Grow as your own person
- Have other friends
- Express your feelings and have them respected
- Decide if and when you want to have sex
- Have your needs be as important as your partner's
- Hold your partner responsible for his or her behavior as you are responsible for yours
- Ask for what you want without being attacked for it
- Be free from abuse.

Anyone who will not accept those rights is being abusive. If he or she demands an equal relationship and these needs aren't met, the relationship isn't worth it.

Guideline #3: Be aware of the danger signs.

If a guy asked a girl out for the first time by saying, "You're going out with me or I'll break your arm!" of course she wouldn't go. Abuse in a relationship doesn't start that way. It builds up over time. That's why it's important to see it coming.

Not all abusive people are alike, but they usually have at least several things in common. Watch out for these signs:

- A bad temper, even though it isn't aimed at you
- A lack of respect for the opposite sex
- The person puts people down a lot
- The person says he or she wants to "take care" of you
- The person has been known to fight with others over past relationships
- All emotions come out as anger
- He or she always blames mistakes on other people
- The person is often moody and tense
- The person doesn't like to lose at anything
- He or she doesn't have close friends.

One or two of those traits are just human nature. If the list fits your partner in four or five ways, you should be careful about going out with him or her.

Guideline #4: Take it slow in any relationship.

It is especially hard to get out of an abusive relationship when the couple has become very

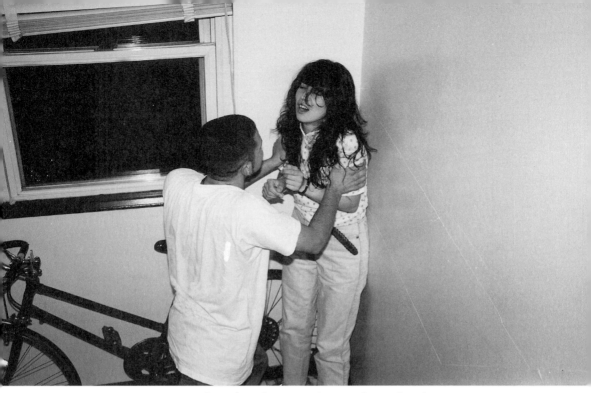

Learn to recognize the danger signs of an abusive relationship. No one has the right to abuse you.

involved. Get to know the person you're dating before getting serious.

A Word About Date Rape

Physical and emotional abuse usually don't happen until a couple has been together for a while. Sexual abuse or date rape can happen on the first date. Knowing that you have the right to say no and behaving safely when on dates are your best defenses against date rape. Don't go to an isolated place with a person you don't know well. State your limits. If your date makes you uncomfortable, call the date off. And even though it may be hard, always tell someone if abuse or rape has occurred.

Chapter 6

What to Do If You're in an Abusive Relationship

Anyone who is trying to get out of a violent relationship needs at least one person to talk to. Feeling alone is one of the things that keeps the abused person hanging on to the relationship.

When an abused person is confused and scared, it's also hard to think of what to do. Someone else can help that person find help.

It's important to find the right person, though. Someone who doesn't understand might say, "You brought it on yourself," or "Why did you stay so long?" The right person is someone who will provide support and respect, not guilt and blame.

Many people turn first to a friend their own age. It's better to tell a friend than no one, but a teenage friend may not have all the information you need.

It's best to find an adult who can really help you. Some turn to their doctor or minister. Teachers,

If you are a victim of abuse, talk to someone whom you trust.

counselors, church youth advisers, and friends' parents are also good choices.

The very best people to help a young person in an abusive relationship are parents. Many teens say, "No! That would be my last resort!" They think their parents will blame them. But parents can be surprising.

Some girls think they will lose all their freedom if they tell their parents. But adults know that everyone needs help now and then. They may want to protect their daughter for a while, but seeing her take sensible steps when she's in trouble will show them that she's growing up.

Others won't turn to their parents because they don't want to upset them. Most parents will be more concerned about their child's safety than about a refusal to obey them.

What if a boy threatens to hurt a girl if she tells her parents? These are often empty threats, but she should tell her parents about the threat.

What if they forbid her to see him again? She can explain that she has to break up with him in her own way. If she presents her case calmly, her parents will be more likely to listen.

If she has never been in this situation before, a girl doesn't know how her parents will react. Or she might know them well enough to know that telling them is not a good idea. In that case, there are still other options:

- Shelters for battered individuals
- Crisis hot lines
- Mental health centers
- Peer counseling groups at school

These are listed in most phone books under Crisis, Battered Women, Family Violence, or Domestic Violence. The operator can also help.

At some point, people in a violent relationship have to break it off. Even with help, that isn't easy. Here are some guidelines put together by people who work with abused women:

- Don't try to break up when you're being attacked. Let things calm down. Then talk.
- Don't hurry. Don't let anyone pressure you.

Take time to think about what you'll say.
- It is okay to break the news over the phone or write a letter. If you want to tell him or her face-to-face, do it in a place with other people around.
- Tell the abuser exactly what he or she has done to drive you away. Be cool and state the facts.
- If you find you just can't say, "It's over," you should at least say that you won't see the person until he or she has gotten help for the problem. That's still a risk, but it lets the abuser know that you won't put up with violence anymore.

If the person doesn't take no for an answer, tell someone right away. Get protection. You are in charge of your life—not your abuser.

Should I Go to the Police?

If going to the police about an abusive partner is frightening to you, perhaps these facts will help you. They come from Jen Rains, a peer speaker for the Youth Outreach Program for the Committee to Aid Abused Women.

A victim of abuse who is under eighteen is usually referred to the youth services division of the police department, where personnel are specially trained. Many of the detectives work with counselors and therapists to provide support.

A girl who goes to the police because she is being abused or battered has several options:

- She can have a police officer let the boy know that there has been a complaint against him. Usually the officer will advise the boy to get help, which often urges him to do so.
- She can file a basic report, which means the boy will not be arrested but the complaint is on record.
- She can press charges against him for assault. If the police believe there are grounds, they will arrest him or turn him over to the juvenile authorities.
- She can ask for a restraining order, which means that if the boy comes near her he will be arrested. However, a girl under eighteen must have her parents make that request.

"Most of the girls I talked to who have gone to the police said the detectives were very positive and supportive," says Jen. "They were very understanding and didn't harass them."

For the One Who Batters

If you have a problem with being violent and you are reading this book, you have taken an important first step. It's hard to admit you do something you haven't been able to control.

But you probably don't know how to stop doing

Emotional abuse—when someone constantly criticizes or insults you—can hurt just as much as physical abuse.

what you're doing. These three things can help you:
1. Admit that you batter.

Even if you say it only to yourself, it helps. If you find yourself saying, "Hey, man, I only slapped her once. What's the big deal?" you haven't owned up to your problem. You have to take that step first.

2. Know that you aren't alone.

You have learned to be violent from our society. Fifty percent of men become violent with a woman at least once. Twenty percent do it often—once a month or more. Seventy-five percent use violent language to control the women in their lives. A lot of people have been helped and healed. You could be one of them.

3. Know that you need to change—and you can.

Your use of violence will only get worse unless you do something about it. If you want to change, you have to go to someone who is trained to help you. That doesn't mean you're weak or a wimp. It means you want to be better than you are.

Find a professional support group. Part of the problem may be that you are isolated and alone. There may not be anyone you can really talk to about your personal feelings.

Most domestic violence programs have groups where men and women can talk honestly and trust each other. In these groups, violent people are taught ways to manage their anger.

You can find groups like these by looking for domestic violence programs in the Yellow Pages of your phone book under Crisis Intervention Services or Social Service Agencies.

Your parents might be able to help you see a private counselor, or you can go to a community mental health center, school counselor, rabbi, minister, or other religious leader.

If you have the right attitude and the right help, you could be well on your way to overcoming your violence problem.

There will always be someone who says, "Every woman needs a good rap in the mouth once in a while!" If you come from a violent family, it will be hard not to fall back into the trap, but it won't be impossible. Work out a life plan that doesn't include violence.

Chapter 7

What to Do for a Friend in an Abusive Relationship

*E*lena's best friend, Mari, had suspected for a long time that Javier was abusing Elena. Once Mari took her arm to get her to look at something, and Elena cried out in pain. Finally Mari saw her bruises and asked her if Javier was hitting her.

When Elena wouldn't answer, Mari decided to take over.

"You have to break up with him, Elena," she said. "I'll go with you if you're afraid."

To her surprise, Elena said, "Just get out of my life! I can handle this myself!"

"No, you can't!" Mari said, "or you wouldn't have those bruises."

Elena turned and walked away.

Several guys knew about Javier's treatment of Elena. Most of them thought, "Hey, if she stays around and takes it, it's her fault as much as it is his. Let them duke it out." But one of Javier's *friends, Shane, didn't see it that way and told Javier to knock it off. Javier decked him and told him to mind his own business.*

If you have tried to help a friend who was in the middle of a violent relationship, you might have been treated as Mari and Shane were.

How can you help someone who doesn't want to be helped?

Most people involved in violence do want help, and there are ways you can get them started in the right direction.

Try not to blame anybody. Don't pile more shame onto what the person is already feeling.

What You Can Do

1. Look up the phone numbers we talked about in Chapter 6 and have them ready. Offer to be with the abused person when she's ready to make the call.

2. Let her talk. Believe her. She may say she wants to try to help her boyfriend. She may say she wants to change herself. Don't try to change her mind. You can help just by listening.

3. It's important not to talk to her boyfriend about it. He might become even angrier with her.

4. Try to get her to talk to an adult she trusts. Although it's helpful for her to talk to you, you shouldn't have to handle this on your own.

5. If you see that she is about to be or already has been injured, call another adult or even the police. That isn't betraying her. That's saving a friend.

6. If you know she's being abused but she hasn't come to you, go to her and gently open the door for her to confide in you. You can say, "Is Phil treating you okay?" Let her know you're there.

What You Can't Do

You can't force her to leave her boyfriend.

You can't make her get help.

You can't force her to take your advice.

You can't be sure that you know what's best for her.

Remember, it's her decision to leave and get help. You can be there to assure her it's the right one.

What to Do to Help a Person Who Batters

It's hard to help a person who is abusive, but you can do some things:

1. Tell him or her you know what's going on.

2. Refuse to accept excuses. Your answer should be, "I don't care why you're doing it. You have no right to abuse somebody."

3. Be prepared to tell him or her where help is available. Provide the phone numbers of people

who can. Offer to go with the person to get help.

4. Suggest that he or she talk to an adult.

5. Even though you don't accept the behavior, let the person know you care.

Even if your efforts to help don't seem to work, hang in there. You are trying to stop a cycle of violence in your generation. And you never know: The little seed you've planted might just grow— and save someone's life.

There's nothing wrong with asking for help in getting over an abusive relationship.

Chapter 8

Breaking the Silence

Breaking up with Dean was the hardest thing Pam thought that she would ever have to do. But she was certain she had made the right decision. Knowing that she wasn't in a situation where Dean could hurt her helped her overcome any feelings of regret.

Pam was angry with Dean. Yet she was also angry with herself for allowing the abuse to occur. Even now that they were broken up, she still thought about him and even missed him. What was wrong with her?

It is simply that Dean and she had shared many new experiences together. Because of him, she'd met a lot of new people and went out more often. Now she had to seek out friends and experiences on her own.

Pam wasn't interested in dating other guys. She was afraid she might never be. After all, she had trusted Dean even after things had started to go wrong.

Pam felt very alone, but she didn't feel comfortable confiding in her friends or family. She needed to talk to someone. The school guidance center gave her the name of a counselor. The counselor encouraged Pam to trust herself and give herself time to heal. Some of his suggestions were:

- Face your fears of being without a boyfriend. Before you get into another relationship, get to know yourself. Think about what you want from a relationship before you start another one.
- Take care of yourself. Do things you like to do and that make you feel good. Be proud because you've done something positive for yourself.

Dean, of course, didn't want to lose Pam. He had strong feelings for her and it was difficult for him to accept that their relationship was really over. Worst of all, it was his fault because he'd hurt Pam. Dean tried to block the situation out of his mind because thinking about it was too painful. He believed that as long as he avoided Pam, things would be okay.

Then, one day before class, a teacher passed him a slip of paper from his guidance counselor. She requested that he stop in during his free period. Dean was annoyed. He was getting good grades and he felt that anything else in his life wasn't the school's business.

When Dean got to the counselor's office, he wanted to tell her to leave him alone. But when he started talking, instead of sounding angry, he sounded scared and sad. Soon, Dean started to cry.

That weekend, Dean joined a program called Break the Cycle. There he realized that unless he did something about his abusive behavior, all his relationships would be the same. He wanted to change and vowed to stay with the program for as long as it took for that to happen.

Like all those who batter and want to get better, Dean had to:

- Accept that it was best for both of them when Pam ended things between them.
- Forgive himself for hurting her. That was over and he could only learn from it. Now he was doing something about it so that he wouldn't hurt anyone again.
- Rebuild his self-esteem. When Dean finally admitted that he had been abusive, he felt really bad about himself. He had to work hard to feel like a good person.
- Believe that his next relationship would be better because he'd learned how to handle his anger, stress, and need for power. He had seen the worst in himself and now had more positive things to look forward to.

Both Pam and Dean had to face difficult realities about themselves and why things went so wrong. The road to recovery was difficult, but it was worth it and both were capable of changing their lives.

Chapter 9

Ending Relationship Violence

Many programs work with schools teaching students strategies to prevent violence and encouraging them to take active roles in ending violence.

At a university in Boston, a group of student-athletes saw a need to start a group for teenagers. The group visits middle and high schools to talk to students about battering, date rape, and sexual harassment. They discuss society's ideas of masculinity and how these may contribute to certain male behaviors.

The group uses a mentor system, spending time with students one on one. The older students are positive role models demonstrating respect and empathy toward others in real-life situations.

This group wants to make teens aware of the role of power in relationships and teach them ways of setting boundaries. This communication helps people

High schools across the country now offer helpful programs and classes on abusive relationships and domestic violence.

solve problems without resorting to violence.

The teens learn to identify early warning signs of abuse. They use skills and strategies to deal with pressure that may lead to violence. They also learn to take responsibility for their actions.

We are all responsible for preventing violence in our society. You can make a difference. Don't be afraid to speak out. You may save someone from getting hurt. Don't accept the mixed messages of television programs and movies that combine sex and violence. Let others know why you won't.

Many cities have dating-abuse prevention programs that visit schools. Request such a program at your school. They are there to help you and your friends. Use them.

Any form of abuse is wrong. Violence is *never* a positive choice.

In Santa Monica, California, there is a program called Break the Cycle. It focuses on educating teens about dating violence and the law. They talk to over 100 students a week and are spreading the word that abusive relationships will not be tolerated and that the future has no place for this kind of behavior. It is up to us to make sure that happens.

Glossary

abuse   Use of force to gain power over another person.

abusive relationship   A relationship in which one or both partners inflict physical, sexual, verbal, or emotional abuse.

battered woman   One whose husband, ex-husband, boyfriend, or lover abuses her over and over again.

date rape   Sexual abuse by a date, partner, or acquaintance that includes sexual intercourse.

domestic violence   Abuse of any kind that happens in the family or home.

emotional abuse   Any action meant to cause fear in another person and eventually destroy self-esteem.

sexual abuse   Force used to make a person do something sexually that the person does not want to do.

Where to Go for Help

Break the Cycle
P.O. Box 1797
Santa Monica, CA 90406-1797
(888) 988-8336
Web site: http://www.wsin.com/btc

Emerge
2830 Massachusetts Avenue, Suite 101
Cambridge, MA 02141
(617) 422-1550
(for men who batter)

Empower Program
6925 Willow Street NW, Suite 228
Washington, DC 20012
(202) 882-2800
Web site: http://www.empowered.org

National Hotline for Battered Women
(800) 621-HOPE (4673)

Teen Dating Intervention Project
2830 Massachusetts Avenue, Suite 101
Cambridge, MA 02141
(617) 354-2676

In Canada

Ottawa Sexual Assault Centre Hotline
(613) 234-2266

For Further Reading

Hicks, John. *Dating Violence: True Stories of Hurt and Hope.* Brookfield, CT: Millbrook Press, 1996.

Johnson, S. A. *When "I Love You" Turns Violent: Emotional and Physical Abuse in Dating Relationships.* Far Hills, NJ: New Horizon Press, 1993.

Kinstlinger-Bruhn, Charlotte. *Everything You Need to Know About Breaking the Cycle of Domestic Violence.* New York: Rosen Publishing Group, 1997.

Levy, Barrie, ed. *Dating Violence: Young Women in Danger.* Seattle, WA: Seal Press, 1998.

Levy, Barrie. *In Love and In Danger: A Teen's Guide to Breaking Free of Abusive Relationships.* Seattle, WA: Seal Press, 1998.

Index

About the Author
Nancy Rue has written two previous books on dating violence.
She has worked with teenagers for twenty-two years as a
teacher, theater director, and youth group leader. She lives with
her husband and daughter in Nevada.

Photo Credits
Cover, p. 33 by Michael Brandt; p. 17 by John Novajosky; p. 57
by Katherine Hsu; p. 58 by Marcus Schaffer; all other photos
by Maria Moreno.

St. Margaret Middle School Library
1716-A Churchville Road
Bel Air, Maryland 21015